# Counting
# The
# Seasons

**Heather E. Schwartz**

**Publishing Credits**

Rachelle Cracchiolo, M.S.Ed., *Publisher*
Conni Medina, M.A.Ed., *Managing Editor*
Nika Fabienke, Ed.D., *Series Developer*
June Kikuchi, *Content Director*
John Leach, *Assistant Editor*
Kevin Pham, *Graphic Designer*

TIME FOR KIDS and the TIME FOR KIDS logo are registered trademarks of TIME Inc. Used under license.

**Image Credits:** All images from from iStock and/or Shutterstock.

**Library of Congress Cataloging-in-Publication Data**

Names: Schwartz, Heather E., author.
Title: Counting : the seasons / Heather E. Schwartz.
Other titles: Seasons
Description: Huntington Beach, CA : Teacher Created Materials, [2018] | Audience: K to grade 3.
Identifiers: LCCN 2017026878 (print) | LCCN 2017029187 (ebook) | ISBN 9781425853297 (eBook) | ISBN 9781425849559 (pbk.)
Subjects: LCSH: Counting--Juvenile literature. | Seasons--Juvenile literature.
Classification: LCC QA113 (ebook) | LCC QA113 .S3925 2018 (print) | DDC 508.2--dc23
LC record available at https://lccn.loc.gov/2017026878

**Teacher Created Materials**
5301 Oceanus Drive
Huntington Beach, CA 92649-1030
http://www.tcmpub.com
**ISBN 978-1-4258-4955-9**
© 2018 Teacher Created Materials, Inc.

winter · spring · fall · summer

Each year has four seasons.
They are **winter**, **spring**, **summer**, and **fall**.

Winter brings three months of cold. Build a snowman. Ride a sled.

Spring brings three months of warm sun.

Smell the flowers.
See them grow.

Summer brings
three months of
heat.
Play outside.
Ride a bike.

Fall brings three months of falling leaves.

Touch the leaves.
See the colors.

There are four seasons.
Each season is three months long.

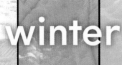
winter

spring

summer

fall

Each year, the four seasons repeat.
Look outside.
Which season is it?

# Glossary

fall

spring

summer

winter